DISCARD

BEING HEALTHY
Meat and Alternatives

Heather C. Hudak

Weigl

CALGARY
www.weigl.com

Published by Weigl Educational Publishers Limited
6325 10 Street S.E.
Calgary, Alberta, Canada
T2H 2Z9

Website: www.weigl.com

Library and Archives Canada Cataloguing in Publication data available upon request.
Fax (403) 233-7769 for the attention of the Publishing Records department.

ISBN 978-1-55388-422-4 (hard cover)
ISBN 978-1-55388-423-1 (soft cover)

Printed in the United States of America
1 2 3 4 5 6 7 8 9 0 12 11 10 09 08

Editor: Heather C. Hudak
Design: Kathryn Livingstone, Terry Paulhus

We gratefully acknowledge the financial support of the Government of Canada
through the Book Publishing Industry Development Program (BPIDP) for our
publishing activities.

Contents

You Are What You Eat

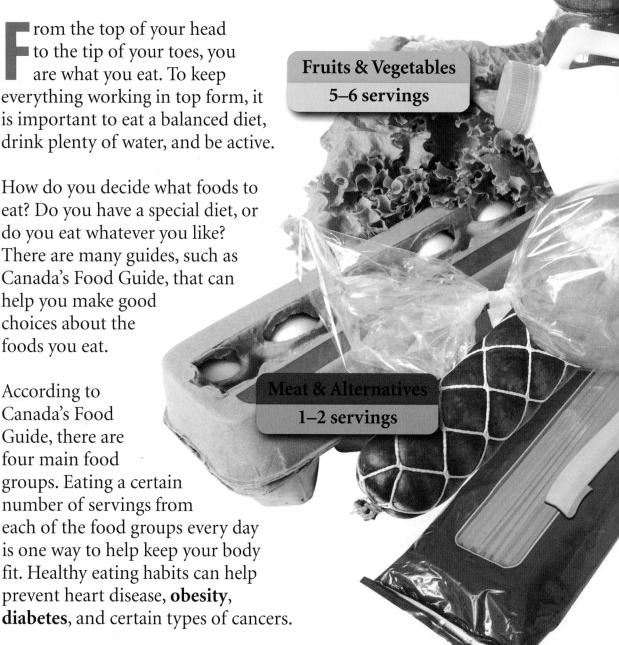

Fruits & Vegetables
5–6 servings

Meat & Alternatives
1–2 servings

From the top of your head to the tip of your toes, you are what you eat. To keep everything working in top form, it is important to eat a balanced diet, drink plenty of water, and be active.

How do you decide what foods to eat? Do you have a special diet, or do you eat whatever you like? There are many guides, such as Canada's Food Guide, that can help you make good choices about the foods you eat.

According to Canada's Food Guide, there are four main food groups. Eating a certain number of servings from each of the food groups every day is one way to help keep your body fit. Healthy eating habits can help prevent heart disease, **obesity**, **diabetes**, and certain types of cancers.

Canadian Food Guide
Recommended Daily Servings for Ages 4-13

Milk & Alternatives
2–4 servings

Grain Products
4–6 servings

Food for Thought

Think about the foods you ate today. How do your eating habits compare to those of other people?

Only 50 percent of Canadian children aged 4 to 18 eat the minimum recommended servings of fruits and vegetables each day.

Thirty percent of Canadian children have at least one soft drink each day.

About 75 percent of children in Canada do not eat the recommended number of grain products.

In Canada, nearly 30 percent of children eat French fries at least twice a week.

More About Meat and Alternatives

From fish to beef and lentils to beans, chances are, you eat some type of meat or meat alternative every day. Take a look at the palm of your hand. This is about how much meat you should eat each day to keep fit.

Think about your lunch today. Did you have a tuna, peanut butter, or bologna sandwich? At breakfast, you may have had bacon or eggs. Beans are a common dinnertime side dish. All of these foods fall into the meat and alternatives food group.

Meat and alternatives consist of a variety of foods that are rich in **protein**, **fat**, iron, zinc, magnesium and B vitamins. A serving size of red meats, fish, and poultry is 125 millilitres.

Types of Meat and Alternatives

Beef

Fish

Nuts

Beans

Eggs

Food for Thought

How can you tell which meats are healthiest?

Lean meats with little fat are healthiest. When buying lean meats, look for labels that use the words "loin" or "round."

Fried meats are full of fats and grease. For a healthier option, eat meats that are **broiled**, grilled, or baked.

From Ocean to Plate

Fish is the main source of animal protein for more than one billion people around the world. Eating two servings of fish each week is a great way to ensure you are making healthy meat choices. Fish have essential oils and are lower in fat than many other meats. They contain **omega 3 fatty acids** that are great for heart health. Salmon, trout, herring, char, and sardines are especially good for you. Shellfish, such as crab and lobster, also count as a fish dish.

Bringing in a Catch

1 To catch fish, fishers cast lines or set nets and traps out at sea.

4 Other fish are cut into **filets** and set in a bed of ice at stores.

2 They bring in their catch and bring it back to shore.

5 Drying and salting fish can help keep it from spoiling longer.

3 Some fish are sent in tanks to marketplaces.

6 Some fish are processed into fish sticks or other meals. Tuna, salmon, and sardines are often cooked and canned.

Cows and Chickens

Barbecuing steak or burgers is a great summertime treat. It is also a good way to grill red meats. Red meats come from the tissue or muscle of adult mammals. This includes mutton and livestock, such as cows. Whether this meat is raw or cooked, it is red in colour.

Red meats are rich in a number of nutrients, such as zinc, protein, and vitamin B12, that help keep your body healthy. However, red meats also contain a great deal of fat. It is important to limit the amount of red meat in your diet to the recommended servings and serving sizes to ensure the best health benefits.

Poultry is an excellent alternative to red meats. Poultry comes from chickens, ducks, turkeys, and geese that are raised for their meat or eggs. Choosing poultry products that are ground or skinless are healthier choices.

Food for Thought

What are red and white meats?

A good way to get **alpha lipoic acid** is by eating red meats.

Pork is sometimes considered a white meat. This is because although it is red when it is raw, it turns white when cooked.

Red meat has fatty acids that can help prevent heart disease.

Red meats have large amounts of iron. Almost all living things need iron to live.

Get the Facts on Nutrition
Learn how to read a food label

When looking for meat products, it is important to read the ingredient list on the food you are buying to check its nutritional value.

The Nutrition Facts table will include the list of **calories** and 13 nutrients.

Nutrition Facts

Serving Size 1 Cake (43g)
Servings Per Container 5

Amount Per Serving

Calories 200 Calories from Fat 90

	% Daily Value*
Total Fat 10g	15%
Saturated Fat 5g	25%
Trans Fat 0g	
Cholesterol 0mg	0%
Sodium 100mg	4%
Total Carbohydrate 26g	9%
Dietary Fiber 0g	0%
Sugars 19g	
Protein 1g	

Vitamin A 0%	•	Vitamin C 0%
Calcium 0%	•	Iron 2%

* Percent Daily Values are based on a 2,000 calorie diet. Your daily values may be higher or lower depending on your calorie needs:

	Calories:	2,000	2,500
Total Fat	Less than	65g	80g
Sat. Fat	Less than	20g	25g
Cholesterol	Less than	300mg	300mg
Sodium	Less than	2,400mg	2,400mg
Total Carbohydrate		300g	375g
Dietary Fiber		25g	30g

1 The facts tell you the serving size and the number of servings in the package. The size of the serving determines the number of calories.

2 Calories tell you how much energy you will get from a serving. Children who get at least one hour of exercise each day should eat between 1,700 and 1,800 calories every day.

3 The first nutrients listed are fats. It is important to limit the number of fats you eat each day.

4 The next nutrients listed are fibre, vitamins, and minerals. These are the parts of food that keep your body healthy and in great shape.

5 The % Daily Value shows how much of the nutrients you need are in one serving of food.

6 The footnote information at the bottom of the label further explains the calorie, nutrient, and % Daily Value information.

Pods to Peanuts

In addition to eating lean meats and fish, you should supplement your diet with alternatives, such as beans, nuts, and tofu. You can even try having one of these alternatives as a main dish instead of meat or fish.

Beans, lentils, peanuts, and peas belong to a family of vegetables called legumes. Most legumes are low fat and have no cholesterol. They have large amounts of protein, potassium, magnesium, folic acid, and iron. Legumes come from a special type of plant. The fruit of this plant is called a pod.

Tofu is made from curdled soy milk that has been pressed into blocks. Naturally, tofu has very little flavour or scent. It can be used in many different food dishes as a good source of iron and protein. Like legumes, it has no fat or cholesterol.

Food for Thought

Why are iron and B vitamins important to your health?

B vitamins, such as thiamin, riboflavin, niacin, and folic acid, help the body release energy from fat, protein, and **carbohydrates**.

Iron carries oxygen in the blood. Without enough iron, your body may feel tired.

12

Comparing Meat Products

Your body needs a certain amount of fats, carbohydrates, and protein to keep it powered. It is important to find the right balance. If a person eats 1,800 calories each day, about 203 to 293 grams should come from carbohydrates, 40 to 70 grams from fats, and 60 to 158 grams from protein. This chart shows the calories, carbohydrate, fat, and protein content of some basic foods.

Product	Alternative
Minced cod fish sticks 210 calories, 9 grams fat, 17 grams carbohydrates, 12 grams protein	**Cooked cod** 105 calories, 1 gram fat, 0 gram carbohydrates, 23 grams protein
Raw kidney beans 337 calories, 1 gram fat, 61 grams carbohydrates, 23 grams protein	**Canned kidney beans** 84 calories, 0 gram fat, 16 grams carbohydrates, 5 grams protein
70 percent lean ground beef 332 calories, 30 grams fat, 0 gram carbohydrates, 14 grams protein	**95 percent lean ground beef** 137 calories, 5 grams fat, 0 gram carbohydrates, 21 grams protein
Fried chicken breast 380 calories, 19 grams fat, 11 grams carbohydrates, 40 grams protein	**Skinless, roasted chicken breast** 120 calories, 11 grams fat, 0 gram carbohydrates, 24 grams protein

Vegetarians are people who do not eat meat. They get their protein from alternative food sources.

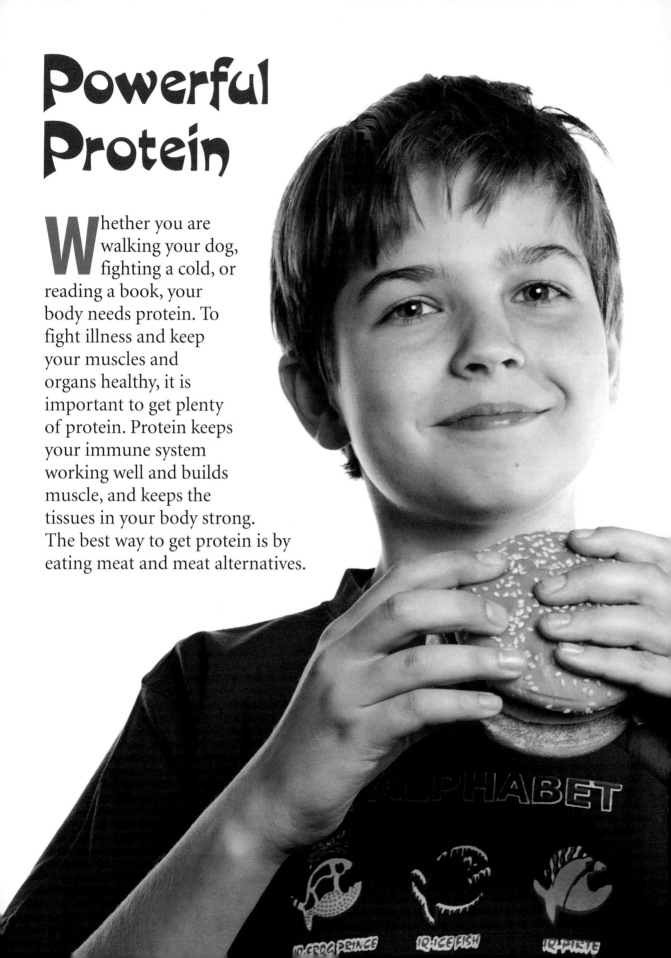

Powerful Protein

Whether you are walking your dog, fighting a cold, or reading a book, your body needs protein. To fight illness and keep your muscles and organs healthy, it is important to get plenty of protein. Protein keeps your immune system working well and builds muscle, and keeps the tissues in your body strong. The best way to get protein is by eating meat and meat alternatives.

What Are Amino Acids?
Learn how your body makes amino acids

Inside your stomach and intestine, special digestive juices break down protein from food into amino acids. These acids make up the protein your body needs to function well. Your body needs 22 types of amino acids. It can make more than half of these on its own, but you must eat foods that are high in protein to get the nine "essential" amino acids that your body cannot produce. To make sure you get enough protein each day, your body needs 1 gram of protein for every 2 pounds that you weigh.

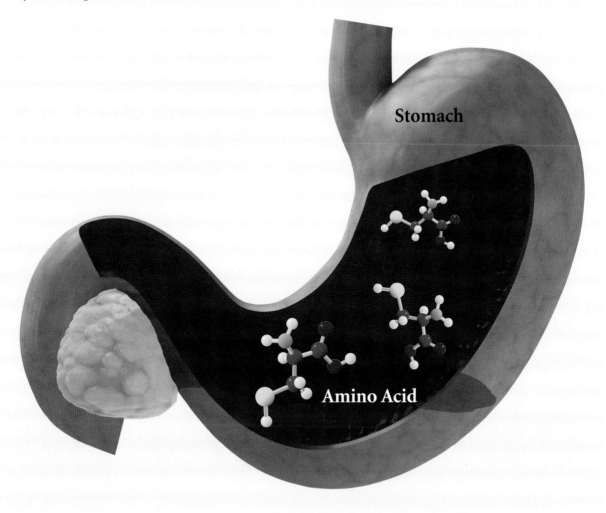

Stomach

Amino Acid

Are You Being Served?

Eating the right foods and enough of them each day will help you get the vitamins and nutrients you need to stay in great shape. Children ages 4 to 13 should have 1 to 2 servings of meat and alternatives daily.

Why not try having an "alternative" dish as a main course instead of meat or fish?

Try using the foods below to plan a daily serving of meat and alternatives. Then, mix and match items to prepare your meat and alternatives servings for one week.

2 eggs

peanut butter (30 millilitres)

tofu (150 grams)

deli meat (125 millilitres)

canned salmon (125 millilitres)

Counting Servings in a Meal

Check out the servings in a meal with fresh bread, chicken, vegetables, a glass of milk, and an orange for dessert.

250 mL (1 cup) vegetables ➤	**2 Fruit & Vegetables** Food Guide Servings
125 mL chicken breast ➤	**1 Meat & Alternatives** Food Guide Servings
1 slice rye bread ➤	**1 Grain Products** Food Guide Servings
250 mL 1% milk ➤	**1 Milk & Alternatives** Food Guide Servings
1 orange ➤	**1 Fruit & Vegetables** Food Guide Servings

shelled seeds (60 millilitres)   **cooked beans** (125 millilitres)   **beef** (125 millilitres)   **ham** (125 millilitres)   **hummus** (125 millilitres)

Fitness Fun

Healthy eating is just part of keeping your body in top form. In Canada, more than 50 percent of boys and 60 percent of girls do not get enough physical activity. From walking to playing team sports or riding a bike, there are many ways to get the physical activity you need each day.

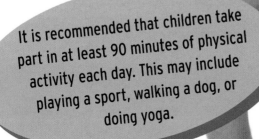

It is recommended that children take part in at least 90 minutes of physical activity each day. This may include playing a sport, walking a dog, or doing yoga.

Food and Fitness Facts

 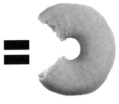

Walking for 22 minutes will burn half of a doughnut.

Thirty minutes of climbing stairs burns a small serving of French fries.

Spending 13 minutes on a bike burns off a glass of pop.

It takes 18 minutes of gardening to burn off 25 peanuts.

WORK ON THIS

If you ate a doughnut, fries, and a pop today, how much would you have to work out to burn off those calories so that you did not gain weight?

Answer: 65 minutes

Calories and Consumption

Your body needs energy to operate. Food provides this energy. A calorie is a unit of energy. Calories are used to measure the amount of potential energy foods have if they are used by your body. A gram of carbohydrates or protein has 4 calories, while a gram of fat contains 9 calories. Your body needs a certain amount of calories each day to function well. If you eat fewer calories than your body requires, you may lose weight. If you eat more calories, you may gain weight. To maintain your weight, you need to burn as many calories as you eat. To burn calories, you need to do physical activity.

Time to Dine

Bean Dip

What you will need

2 tablespoons
  olive oil
0.25 cup of diced
  red peppers
0.125 cup pepper
  and dried parsley

0.25 teaspoon of
  dried basil, thyme,
  rosemary, and salt
1 garlic clove
2 tablespoons
  lemon juice

15-ounce can
  of drained
  white beans
blender
spatula
bowl

What to do

1. Place all of the ingredients, except the red pepper,
   in the blender.
2. Blend until smooth.
3. Pour the blended mixture into a bowl.
4. Stir in the red peppers, and serve.

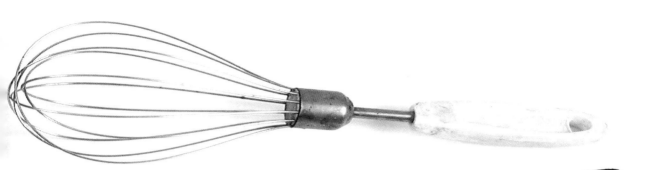

Beef Kabobs

What you will need

1 pound sirloin
  or round cut
  beef cubes
2 tablespoons
  olive oil

1 garlic clove
1 teaspoon
  paprika
1 onion
1 green pepper

water
sandwich bag
wooden skewers
small knife
barbecue

What to do

1. Place the beef cubes, garlic, paprika, and olive oil in the sandwich bag. Seal the bag, and place it in the fridge for at least two hours.
2. With an adult's help, cut the pepper and the onion into wedges.
3. Soak the skewers in water for about 30 minutes.
4. Remove the beef from the fridge, and put one cube on a wooden skewer. Next, place an onion and a pepper wedge on the skewer. Repeat, alternating the beef, onion, and pepper, until the skewer is full.
5. Have an adult grill the skewers on a barbecue until the beef is very brown.
6. Remove from the grill, let cool, and enjoy.

What Have You Learned?

What is red meat?

Answer: the tissue or muscle of adult mammals

What are the four food groups?

Answer: Fruits and Vegetables Milk and Alternatives Meat and Alternatives Grain Products

How is tofu made?

Answer: from curdled soy milk that is pressed together into blocks

What are legumes?

Answer: a special type of plant with a fruit called a pod

Where does poultry come from?

Answer: chicken, turkey, duck, goose

How can you burn off half a doughnut?

Answer: walk for 22 minutes

Further Research

How can I find out more about meat and healthy eating?

Most libraries have computers that connect to a database that contains information on books and articles about different subjects. You can input a key word and find material on that person, place, or thing you want to learn more about. The computer will provide you with a list of books in the library that contain information on the subject you searched for. Non-fiction books are arranged numerically, using their call number. Fiction books are organized alphabetically by the author's last name.

Websites

For a copy of Canada's Food Guide, surf to
www.hc-sc.gc.ca/fn-an/food-guide-aliment/index-eng.php.

To learn more about healthy living, download the guide at
www.healthycanadians.gc.ca/pa-ap/cg-cg_e.html.

For information about your body, fitness, food and other health topics, visit
http://kidshealth.org/kid.

Glossary

alpha lipoic acid: a substance found in the body which helps maintain normal nerve function

broiled: cooked by direct heat, as on a grill or in an oven

calories: units of measure for the amount of heat made by a food when it is used by the body

carbohydrates: compounds made of carbon, hydrogen, and oxygen; sugars and starches

diabetes: a disease in which the body has too much blood sugar; treated with insulin, a substance that controls the use of sugar by the body

fat: an oily or greasy substance that is found naturally in animal products

filets: pieces of meat or fish that have bones removed

obesity: very overweight

omega 3 fatty acids: a kind of healthy fat found in leafy green vegetables, vegetable oils, and fish

protein: a substance that is needed by all living things

Index